Fact!

A double cheeseburger has 25 grams of fat, while a hamburger has 10 grams of fat. A gram of fat is equal to 9 calories.

If you choose to eat a double cheese-burger instead of a hamburger, how many more calories of fat will you be eating?

3

135 calories

Level 2

Weird!

Rosie the Ribeteer holds the record for longest leap for a bullfrog. She jumped 21 feet 5 ¾ inches.

If Rosie made practice jumps of 20, 16, and 12 feet, what was the average length of her practice jumps?

16 feet

4

MATH
CHALLENGE

190
Fun and Creative
Problems for Kids

LEVEL 2

James Riley, Ph.D., Marge Eberts, Ed.S.,
and Peggy Gisler, Ed.S.

GOOD YEAR BOOKS

are available for most basic curriculum subjects plus many enrichment
areas. For more Good Year Books, contact your local bookseller or
educational dealer. For a complete catalog with information about
other Good Year Books, please contact:

Good Year Books
P.O. Box 91858
Tucson, AZ 85752-1858
www.goodyearbooks.com

ISBN: 1-59647-026-7

Illustrations: Slug Signorino
Design: Daniel Miedaner

Fact!

Alan Shepard was the first American in space. The rocket that carried him into space used up 1 gallon of fuel for every 60 feet of height it gained.

Could the rocket have gone 1 mile on 88 gallons of fuel?

ǝlᴉɯ ⇂ ʎlʇɔɐxǝ 'sǝʎ

Neat!

About every 74 minutes, Old Faithful in Yellowstone National Park blows thousands of gallons of water from 100 to 180 feet into the air.

What is the average height of water that Old Faithful blows into the air?

6

140 feet

Really?

The amount of food Tyrannosaurus rex ate in 1 bite is equal to the amount a family of 4 would eat in a month. The average cost for that much food is $463.

How much would it cost to feed Tyrannosaurus rex 3 bites of food?

7

$1,389

Listen!

Phillis Wheatley came to America on a slave ship when she was 8. She became a famous poet and was first published in 1773.

If Phillis was born in 1753, in what year was she brought to America? How old was she in 1773?

8

1761, 20 years old

Who Knew?

In ancient Greece, distances were measured by hiring men to walk in equal steps between towns and count their steps.

If each step was 30 inches long, how many feet would a man have walked in 80 steps?

200 feet

9

Weird!

In 1930, two men drove a car backward 3,340 miles from New York to Los Angeles and then back to New York. They drove 7,180 miles total.

How many miles longer was their return trip to New York than the trip to Los Angeles?

10

500 miles

Look!

The telescope at Mount Palomar in California is one of the world's largest. The telescope's mirror has a hole in the middle 40 inches in diameter.

Could someone 4 feet tall stand in the hole?

11

no, he or she would be 8 inches too tall

Fact!

Abraham Lincoln was our tallest president, at 6 feet 4 inches tall. James Madison was the shortest president, at 5 feet 4 inches tall.

How much taller was Lincoln than Madison? What is the average of their heights?

12 inches, 5 feet 10 inches

12

Really?

The bird with the most feathers is the whistling swan. It has 25,216 feathers, of which 20,177 are found on its head and neck.

How many feathers does the swan have on the rest of its body?

13

5,039 feathers

Cool!

A housefly can fly about 5 miles per hour, a bee can fly about 14 miles per hour, and a blue jay can fly about 20 miles per hour.

About how many times faster can a bee fly than a housefly? About how many times faster can a blue jay fly than a housefly?

about 3, about 4

14

Fact!

The blast from the Tambora volcano in 1815 lowered the height of the 13,450-foot volcano by 4,100 feet.

What was the height of Mount Tambora after the blast?

15

9,350 feet

Look!

From the first trip to the moon, Neil Armstrong and Buzz Aldrin brought back about 47 pounds of lunar rocks.

Objects on the moon weigh 6 times less than they do on Earth. How much did the rocks weigh on the moon?

about 8 pounds

16

Weird!

King Henry I of England ordered that the unit of measure called a foot be equal to $\frac{1}{3}$ of the length of his arm, which was 36 inches long.

If King Henry's arm had been 42 inches long, how long would a foot be?

17

14 inches

Really?

Anteaters sleep during the day and come out and catch ants only after dark.

If an anteater eats 3,209 ants on Monday, 2,165 ants on Tuesday, and 1,986 ants on Wednesday, how many ants must he eat on Thursday to have eaten 10,000 ants in 4 days?

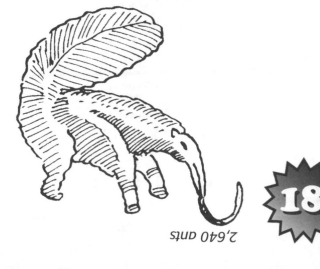

2,640 ants

18

What If?

In the United States, the average woman is about 5 feet 4 inches tall. An average man is about 5 feet 8 inches tall.

If Jeff is 5 inches taller than Shannah, and Shannah is 3 inches under average height for a woman, how tall is each?

Jeff is 5 feet 6 inches tall, Shannah is 5 feet 1 inch tall

Look!

The Dog Star, the brightest star you can see, is 8.64 light-years away. Alpha Centauri, the nearest star you can see, is 4.35 light-years away.

How much closer to the Earth is Alpha Centauri than the Dog Star?

4.29 light-years

20

Listen!

Greenland isn't very green! The Viking Eric the Red gave Greenland its name to make people want to live there, but ice covers 0.85 of the land.

How much of Greenland is green?

21

0.15 or 15%

Who Knew?

The most rain that ever fell in a year in the United States was 739 inches at Kukui on Maui, Hawaii.

What was the average rainfall per month?

22

62 inches

Really?

In 1974, scientists sent a 3-minute message describing the Earth and its people to any life in the Hercules Constellation. So far, no one has answered the message.

What fraction of an hour is the 3-minute message?

23

³/₆₀ **or** ¹/₂₀

Cool!

The bumblebee bat is the smallest land mammal. It weighs about 2 grams, the weight of 2 large paper clips.

How many bumblebee bats would it take to weigh 1 kilogram?

500 bumblebee bats

24

What If?

The Monterey Bay Aquarium is one of the biggest aquariums in the world.

If admission rates are $19.95 for adults, $15.95 for ages 13–17, and $8.95 for ages 3–12, how much will admission cost for Mom, Dad, 9-year-old Carlos, and 14-year-old Maria?

$64.80

Who Knew?

A golf hole is 4.25 inches in diameter and 4 inches deep. A hockey puck is 3 inches in diameter and 1 inch thick.

Will a hockey puck fit into a golf hole? If so, how much room will it have to spare?

26

Fact!

A good milk cow will give nearly 6,000 quarts of milk every year.

A quart equals 4 cups. If you drink 3 cups of milk every day, about how many quarts of milk will you drink in a year?

about 274 quarts

Really?

King Ptolemy IV of ancient Egypt built huge ships. His largest ship was powered by sailors pulling on 4,000 oars.

If 8 sailors were needed to pull on each oar, how many people were needed to power the boat?

28

32,000 people were needed

Fact!

The Dead Sea has the most salt of any body of water—280 parts salt per 1,000 parts water. The ocean has about 35 parts per 1,000.

How many times more salt does the Dead Sea have than the ocean?

29

8 times

Fact!

Mercury is the fastest-moving planet. The planet goes around the sun at a speed of 30 miles per second and completes an orbit in 3 months.

How many times does Mercury orbit the sun in one Earth year?

4 times

30

Look!

Almost ½ the people in the United States over 3 years of age wear glasses.

If there are 240 million people over 3 years old in this country, about how many wear glasses?

120 million

Weird!

The longest dragon costume was 3,023 feet long. The dragon danced at the Happy Valley racecourse in Hong Kong.

If people were spaced 3 feet apart underneath the dragon, about how many people were needed to make the dragon dance?

1,008 people

32

Really?

You dream for about $\frac{1}{5}$ of the time that you spend asleep.

If you sleep for 8 hours, about how many minutes do you spend dreaming?

33

96 minutes

Cool!

The Iditarod is a 1,049-mile dog sled race in Alaska. The record, 8 days, 22 hours, 46 minutes, and 2 seconds, belongs to Martin Buser.

Martin raced for almost 9 full days. About how far did he have to travel each day?

116½ miles

34

Look!

The Hoba West meteorite is the heaviest meteorite known to have fallen to the Earth. It weighs about 60 metric tons (1 metric ton = 2,200 pounds).

How many pounds does the meteorite weigh?

35

132,000 pounds

Fact!

The hummingbird, the only bird that can fly backward, has a body temperature of 110° F.

If your body temperature is 98.6° F, how much warmer is the humming-bird's body?

about 11° F

36

What If?

At the Indianapolis 500, 33 racecars zoom around a 2.5 mile track for 200 laps.

A racecar driver has led the race for 50 laps. For how many miles has he led the race?

37

125 miles

Weird!

A swami in India did not sit or lie down for more than 17 years. He did not stop standing until 1973. He even slept leaning against a plank!

What year did the swami begin his record stand?

1956

38

Who Knew?

The blue whale, the largest animal on the Earth, is as long as 3 school buses.

If a blue whale is 93 feet long, how long is a school bus?

39

31 feet

Really?

When the first emperor of China died, he was buried surrounded by clay statues of soldiers and their horses.

If the emperor was surrounded by 200 rows of 7 soldiers, how many soldiers were in this special army?

1,400 soldiers

40

Look!

In 1860, Pony Express riders rode horses from town to town carrying the mail. The postage rate then was 50¢ an ounce.

If a rider carried 2 pounds of mail on a trip, how much postage would have been due?

41

$16.00

Neat!

An elephant can run about 25 miles per hour, while a camel can run only 10 miles per hour.

If an elephant and a camel start running from the same spot, how far ahead will the elephant be in 8 hours?

120 miles

42

Fact!

The Great Pyramid at Giza, Egypt, is 450 feet high. The Statue of Liberty in the New York City Harbor is 190 feet high.

About how many times higher is the pyramid?

43

a little more than twice

Who Knew?

A housefly only lives for 2 weeks.

For how many hours can you expect a housefly to fly around in your house?

336 hours

44

What If?

Catsup was popular as a medicine 150 years ago!

If you buy a 28-ounce bottle of catsup today for $1.12, how many cents does it cost per ounce?

45

$0.04 per ounce

Really?

In 1968, Richard Dodd returned a book his great-grandfather checked out from the University of Cincinnati library in 1823.

If the fine for overdue books was 25¢ a day, about how much might the fine have been for this book?

46

about $13,231

Weird!

A dentist in Rome kept all the teeth he extracted from his patients from 1868 to 1903. There were 2,000,744 teeth in his collection!

What was the average number of teeth he extracted in a day?

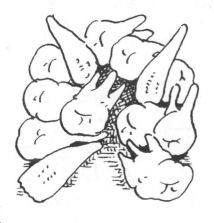

47

Fact!

Rice is the main food for $\frac{1}{2}$ the people of the world.

If there are 6 billion people in the world, about how many million people eat mainly rice?

48

3,000 million

Neat!

News travels fast in your body. Signals move along your nerves at speeds as high as 200 miles per hour.

How many feet do nerve signals travel in an hour? How would you figure out how many feet they travel in a minute?

49

200 miles per hour x 5,280 feet per mile = 1,056,000 feet per hour.
1,056,000 ÷ 60 minutes per hour = 17,600 feet per minute

Really?

Stars can be very heavy! When a star becomes a white dwarf, a spoonful of the star could weigh as much as 10 tons.

How many pounds would that same spoonful weigh?

20,000 pounds

50

Who Knew?

The temple of the Greek goddess Artemis took 220 years to build.

If the temple was begun in 541 B.C., when was it finished? Remember that B.C. year numbers get smaller as they go up!

51

321 B.C.

Look!

On November 23, 1942, an English ship sank in the Atlantic Ocean. Poon Lim, a Chinese sailor, was the only survivor.

Poon Lim drifted in a life raft until he was rescued on April 5, 1943. How many days did he spend in the raft?

52

134 days

Fact!

In the year 600, the Aztec city of Tenochtitlan was one of the biggest in the world. It covered 5 square miles and had a population of 250,000 people.

About how many people lived in each square mile?

53

about 50,000 people

Really?

You have about 100,000 hairs on your head, which grow at the rate of $\frac{1}{100}$ of an inch every day.

If you don't cut your hair, about how much will it grow in a year? In 2 years?

about 3 ½ inches, 7 inches

54

Cool!

In 1972, a scientist discovered dinosaur bones in a plot about 54 feet tall and 89 feet long.

If he had to dig a rectangle around the skeleton to get it out, about how many square feet was the area of the rectangle?

55

about 4,806 square feet (54 x 89)

Weird!

The world's largest ice construction was the Ice Palace built in Minnesota in 1986. It was 13 stories tall and built with 9,000 blocks of ice.

About how many blocks were used for each story?

about 692 blocks per story

56

What If?

Your sister Lisa loves blowing bubbles, so you decide to get her a bottle of bubble mix for her birthday.

If a 10-ounce bottle costs $4.25 and a 20-ounce bottle costs $7.00, which is cheaper per ounce?

57

the 20-ounce bottle

Neat!

Man o' War is one of the greatest American racehorses of all time. He won 20 of the 21 races he ran. The distance racehorses run is measured in furlongs, $\frac{1}{8}$ of a mile.

Would Man o' War have run farther if he ran a race of $1\frac{1}{8}$ miles or of 16 furlongs?

16 furlongs—about 2 miles

58

Really?

The Great Pyramid in Egypt was built by 400,000 workers in just 20 years. At that time the average Egyptian only lived 35 years.

What part of a worker's life was spent building the Great Pyramid?

59

$^{20}/_{35}$ or $^4/_7$

Fact!

Alaska is the largest of the 50 states; Rhode Island is the smallest. Rhode Island is 1,214 square miles, and Alaska is 586,000 square miles.

How many Rhode Islands could fit in Alaska? Use a calculator to find out.

Almost 483 Rhode Islands

60

What If?

You breathe about 70,000 cubic inches of air a day. A cubic foot is 1,728 cubic inches.

If you were in a room that was 10 feet long, 10 feet wide, and 10 feet high, how many days would it take you to breathe all the air in the room?

25, rounded up from 24.6

Weird!

Toby, a New York City poodle, was left $75 million when his owner died in 1931.

If Toby put the money in a savings account that paid him 1% a year in interest, how much would Toby have at the end of the year?

$75,750,000

62

Who Knew?

Did you know that your body is 70% water? You need a lot of water to live and be healthy.

What percentage of your body is not water? What fraction of your body is that?

30%, ³/₁₀ or almost ¹/₃

Fact!

A year on Venus is 225 Earth days long.

Which is longer, an Earth year or a Venus year? By how many weeks is it longer?

Earth year, 20 weeks

64

What If?

You are ordering pizzas for your party of 20 people. A large pizza has 16 slices, a medium has 14, and a small has 10.

If you wanted exactly 2 pieces for each person, what combination of pizzas should you order?

65

a small, medium, and large or 4 smalls

Really?

The shifting of the Earth's continental plates is separating Australia and Hawaii by about 2 ½ inches per year.

About how many feet farther apart will Australia and Hawaii be in 20 years?

about 4

Fact!

You have 27 bones in your hand and wrist, 26 in your foot and ankle, 26 in your spine, and 12 pairs of ribs.

How many other bones are there in the total of 206?

67

50

Really?

You have to use 3,500 calories to lose 1 pound. If you rode a bicycle for 1 hour at 10 mph, you would use 325 calories.

About how many miles would you have to ride to lose 1 pound?

68

about 108 miles

Look!

Fish need space too! In an aquarium, 1 gallon of water will support 2 small fish or 1 large fish.

If you have a 30-gallon aquarium, how many fish can you have in your aquarium if you want an equal number of small and large fish?

20 large and 20 small fish

Listen!

A 1-ounce serving of Spartan Bran Flakes Cereal contains 90 calories. If you add ½ cup of fortified skim milk, the number of calories increases to 130.

How many calories are in a cup of skim milk?

70

80 calories

Look!

In 1877, Giovanni Schiaparelli reported that he saw canals on the surface of Mars. Galileo had reported the same thing 267 years earlier.

In what year did Galileo announce his discovery of canals on Mars?

71

Who Knew?

The first fax machine was invented in 1843. The telephone was patented 33 years later. The first photocopier was made 95 years after the first fax.

In what year was the telephone patented? How many years later was the photo-copier made? In what year?

72

1876, 62, 1938

Neat!

In the Old West, 12 cowboys could move 3,000 cattle a day. They went about 12 miles a day, and traveled $^2/_3$ of this distance in the morning when it was cooler.

How many miles did they move in the afternoon when it was hot?

4 miles

What If?

A baby giraffe is $1\frac{1}{2}$ meters high and weighs 70 kilograms. An adult giraffe is 5 meters high and has gained 830 kilograms.

How many times taller is an adult giraffe than a baby one?
How much does an adult weigh?

74

3.33 times taller, 900 kilograms

Really?

The longest train trip in the world is from Moscow to Nakhodka, Siberia. It is 5,852 miles long and takes 192 hours.

How many days would you be on the train if you took this trip?

75

8 days

Fact!

The average calorie intake in the United States is 3,330 per person per day.

If 4 Americans consumed 11,250 calories in one day, how much did this differ from the national average?

each was 517.5 calories below average

76

Cool!

The top 2 favorite breeds of dogs in 2003 were the Labrador retriever and the golden retriever.

The American Kennel Club has registered 144,934 Labrador retrievers and 52,530 golden retrievers. How many more labs have been registered than goldens?

92,404

Who Knew?

Three horse years are equal to 8 people years. A Morgan horse named Rebel lives in Kalamazoo, Michigan, and is 33 years old. What is Rebel's age in people years?

78

88 years old

What If?

A loaf of whole wheat bread contains 20 slices. A package of sliced turkey ham contains 8 slices.

How many turkey ham sandwiches can be made with 3 loaves of bread and 2 packages of sliced ham?

79

16 sandwiches

Fact!

Colorado is 1 of only 2 states that are almost rectangular in shape. Colorado is about 280 miles long and 370 miles wide.

What is the approximate area of Colorado in square miles? What is the other rectangular state?

about 103,600 square miles,
Wyoming

Listen!

The 30 Years' War lasted from 1618 to 1648, and the 100 Years' War lasted from 1337 to 1453.

How long did these wars actually last?

the 30 Years' War lasted 30 years, the 100 Years' War lasted 116 years

Really?

A scientific study on deer populations showed that a deer needs 15 acres of open space to live on.

A square mile contains 640 acres. About how many deer can live in a square mile?

82

42 deer

Fact!

The coast redwood tree can be as much as 362 feet tall. The fleshy hawthorne can grow to be 8 feet tall.

How many hawthornes will it take end-to-end to be as tall as one coast redwood?

83

about 45 of them

Listen!

The youngest astronaut was Colonel Titov of the USSR, who was 25 when he made his flight. Karl Heinze was the oldest, 33 years older than Titov.

How old was Heinze? If Titov made his flight in 1960, what year was he born?

84

Heinze was 58, Titov was born in 1935

What If?

The first daily weather forecast began in Great Britain in 1861.

The weather forecast reports a 100% chance of 1 day of rain on either Monday, Tuesday, or Wednesday. It didn't rain on Monday. What is the probability that it will rain on Tuesday?

50% probability

Really?

The average time a seal can stay under water is about 30 minutes, but may vary as much as 20 minutes either way.

What are the upper and lower limits on the time a seal can hold its breath under water?

86

50 minutes, 10 minutes

Fact!

A 110-pound person can burn 3.2 calories per minute bicycling, while a 190-pound person will burn 5.5 calories per minute.

How many more calories will the 190-pound person burn in 1 hour than the 110-pound person burns?

87

138 more calories

Fact!

Light travels 186,282 miles per second.

About how many seconds would it take to see a light 800,000 miles away? Estimate using the first 2 digits.

about 4 seconds

88

Who Knew?

In 1820, 71% of all workers, about 2 million, worked on farms. Today only 2.5% of all workers, about 2.8 million, work on farms.

Are more people working on farms today than in 1820?

sǝʎ

Neat!

Ants are good farmers! They herd small insects called aphids and milk them, and also grow fungus to feed their young.

An ant colony has 4 tunnels. If ants randomly enter and leave by any tunnel, what are the chances that they will enter and leave by different tunnels?

3 out of 4

90

What If?

Two mathematicians are talking about their children. The first says, "The product of my daughters' ages is 36. The sum of their ages is 12." The second asks, "How can that be?"

What are the daughters' ages? What is unusual about this?

they're both 6, they're twins

Who Knew?

In South America, a part of the tropical rain forest the size of a football field is cut down about every 3 seconds.

If cutting continues at this rate, how many minutes from now will 100 football fields of rain forest be gone?

5 minutes from now

92

Look!

In ancient cultures, people measured days from the start of a new moon. The word *month* comes from the word *moon.*

There are 12 new moons a year, and 29.5 days from one new moon to the next. How close does 12 moons come to being a year?

93

11 days

What If?

The top speed for a mouse is 8 miles per hour, for a dog, 40 mph, and for a cat, 30 mph.

If a dog, cat, and mouse start running from points 1 mile apart, will the dog catch the cat before the cat catches the mouse?

94

no, the cat will catch the mouse first

Fact!

The maximum duration of a solar eclipse is 7 minutes 31 seconds, while the moon passes between the sun and the Earth.

If the eclipse will begin at 3:34 p.m. and you go out at 15:40 (24-hour time), will you see the eclipse?

95

yes, it's 3:40

A fossil crocodile found in Texas was estimated to be 40–50 feet long!

About how many meters long was this crocodile?

96

12-15 meters

Cool!

Ty Cobb leads Major League players in the number of career runs scored at 2,245. A run is around all 4 bases.

The distance between bases is 90 feet. About how many miles did Ty Cobb run to score his 2,245 runs?

97

about 153 miles

Weird!

Skin is the largest organ of the human body, and it completely replaces itself every 28 days.

About how many times will your skin have replaced itself in a year?

98

about 13 times

Really?

There is really only one huge ocean, which covers 140 million square miles. The Earth's surface is 197,000,000 square miles.

What fraction of the Earth's surface is land?

99

$^7/_{10}$ *or roughly* $^3/_4$ *of the Earth's surface*

Neat!

In 1863, James Plimpton made the first roller skates.

A man named David Frank once roller-skated 270 miles in 37 hours. About how many miles did he skate each hour?

about 7 miles

100

Look!

King Solomon built a house that had a length of 60 cubits, a width of 20 cubits, and a height of 30 cubits.

The ancient measure cubit was about 18 inches. What were the dimensions of King Solomon's house in feet?

101

90 by 30 by 45 feet

Really?

Each day, the average American throws away about 3 1/2 pounds of trash.

How much trash does the average American throw away in a year?

102

1,277.5 pounds of trash

What If?

Milton wants to buy fish for his aquarium. Tiger barbs are $1.00 each, neon tetras are 4/$1.00, angelfish are $1.25, and silver dollars are 2/$1.50.

If Milton wants 2 tiger barbs, 6 neon tetras, 1 angelfish, and 4 silver dollars, how much money will he need?

103

$7.75

Weird!

You are being eaten alive! There are about 300,000 microbes on any ³/₄-inch square of your skin, eating the dead skin cells.

About how many microbes are on a 3-inch square of skin?

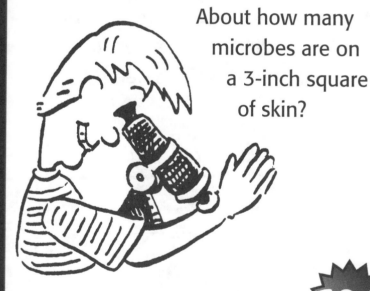

4,800,000 microbes

104

Really?

The largest invertebrate animal is the giant squid, which can be 55 feet long. Its eye alone is 15 inches across.

What percentage of the squid's body length is its eye? Use a calculator and round to the nearest hundredth.

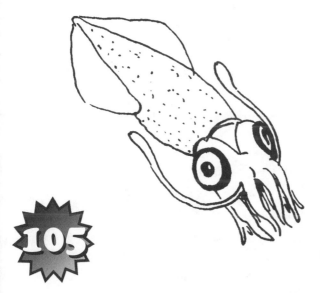

105

2.27%

Look!

The Sahara Desert in Africa gets 4,300 hours of sunshine a year, making it the sunniest place in the world.

Assuming an average of 12 hours of daylight per day, about how many days of sun does the Sahara get in a year? What percentage of the year is sunny?

106

about 358 days, about 98% of the year

Cool!

On April 29, 1978, Naomi Uemura of Japan became the first person to dogsled to the North Pole alone. It took him 58 days to make the 500-mile trip.

On what day did Naomi start his trip? On average, how many miles did he travel each day?

107

March 2, 8.62 miles

 math challenge

Level 2

Really?

About 20,000,000 people moved to the United States between 1892 and 1943 because of trouble in their countries.

On average, how many people immigrated each year? Round the number to the nearest one.

108

392,157 people

Fact!

The diameter of the Earth is only 7,927 miles, whereas the diameter of Jupiter is 88,734 miles.

Use a calculator to find out how many times larger Jupiter is.

109

about 11 times

Weird!

The nephila spider spins a web 6 feet across. A single thread can be 20 feet long. The spider can spin 370 feet of silk in an hour.

How many hours would it take the spider to spin a mile of silk? Use a calculator.

over 14 hours (about 14 1/4)

110

Cool!

In the 1924 Olympics, Thorleif Haug of Norway skied 50 kilometers in 3 hours 44 minutes. In 1994, Vladimir Smirnov of Kazakhstan won in 2 hours 7 minutes.

How many minutes longer did it take Haug to complete the course than it did Smirnov?

97 minutes

Look!

The San Andreas Fault in California runs for 600 miles along the coast. Los Angeles and San Francisco are 600 kilometers apart.

Is the fault longer or shorter than the distance between L.A. and San Francisco?

the fault is longer, by about 200 miles

112

What If?

Tony is shopping for a present for his brother's birthday. He sees a space-ship building kit, which is $15.00, but he only has $13.00.

Tony notices a sign saying that all building kits are on sale for 20% off. Can he afford the kit?

yes, it's $12.00 on sale

Who Knew?

The highest waterfall in the world is Angel Falls in Venezuela. It is over 979 meters high.

About how high is Angel Falls in feet?

about 3,200 feet

114

Really?

One hundred-year-old eagle nests have been found that are 20 feet high and 10 feet across and weigh 2 tons.

On average, about how many pounds are added each year? About how many inches taller is the nest each year?

*40 pounds heavier and
2 ²/₅ inches higher*

Listen!

If you cut a plant into sections and put one end of each in water, new plants will grow from the cuttings.

Four 9-inch plants are cut into 3-inch sections and planted. How many total plants might grow?

12 plants

Fact!

The dinosaur Stegosaurus weighed 15,000 times the weight of its brain. Its brain weighed 4 ounces.

What was the weight of a Stegosaurus in pounds?

117

3,750 pounds

Cool!

Chocolate is made from beans from cacao trees. Each tree usually has 30 pods, each of which has 20 to 40 beans.

What is the maximum number of beans you could expect from 1 tree? What is the minimum? What is the average?

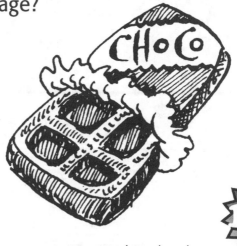

118

1,200; 600; 900 beans

What If?

Imagine you are on vacation in Florida, and you want to buy postcards for all your friends.

If each postcard costs $1.15 with tax, how many can you buy if you have $6.50?

5 postcards

Really?

The shortest river in the world is the Roe River in Montana, which is 200 feet long. One of the longest rivers is the Nile in Africa which is 4,160 miles long.

How many times longer is the Nile than the Roe?

109,824 times

120

Who Knew?

The Croton Egg Farm in Ohio has 4.8 million hens laying 3.7 million eggs a day. That is 308,333 dozen eggs.

If a chicken and a half can lay an egg and a half in a day and a half, how many eggs will 3 chickens lay in 3 days?

121

6 eggs

Really?

Blondes have about 140,000 hairs on their heads. Redheads have about 90,000. People with black or brown hair have about 5,000 fewer hairs than the average of these two.

About how many hairs does someone with black or brown hair have?

122

about 110,000

Look!

The largest cactus in the United States is the saguaro. The saguaro can live for 200 years.

If a saguaro cactus grows 2.7 inches a year, how tall will it be in 200 years?

123

45 feet tall

Fact!

A good way to estimate the circumference of a circle is to multiply the diameter by 3.

The diameter of the Earth is about 7,900 miles. What is the estimated length of a circular orbit of a satellite that is 500 miles above the Earth?

124

25,200 miles

Really?

In 1961, Victor Prather and Malcolm Ross of the U.S. Navy reached an altitude of 113,740 feet in a balloon. This is so high they had to wear space suits.

How many miles high did Prather and Ross go in their balloon?

125

about 21 ½ miles

Fact!

In the mountains, the air temperature drops an average of 1° F for every 300-foot increase in height.

If the temperature is 72° F at the base, what is the temperature 3,600 feet up on the mountain slope?

60° F

126

Listen!

Bison live 15 years, moose live 12 years.

A zoo got a baby moose and a baby bison. The moose lived 12 years. When the moose died, what fraction of its life did the bison have yet to live?

127

$^3/_{15} = {}^1/_5$ of its life

Neat!

Jamaica spice fruitcake includes raisins, figs, almonds, dates, glazed cherries, and orange peel. The batter from one recipe fills 2 bread pans, each 9 x 5 x 3 inches.

What should the recipe be multiplied by to fill 2 pans, each 10 x 9 x 3 inches?

128

2 times

Listen!

Sound travels about 738 mph through air, but about 11,160 mph through steel.

About how many times faster will you hear something a mile away through a steel wire than through air?

129

about 15 times faster

Who Knew?

The average adult has 18 square feet of skin and 206 bones.

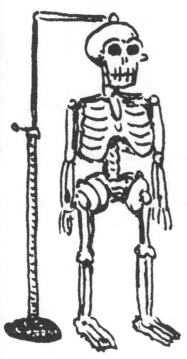

A 160-pound man has about 6 pounds of skin. 1 pound in 5 of a man's weight is bone. How many pounds of skin and bones does a 160-pound man have?

spunod 8ε

130

Look!

Only ²/₃ of the people who live in Estonia today are Estonian, and ¹/₃ of them are Russians.

If ¹/₂ of the Russians who now live in Estonia went back to Russia, what fraction of the people living in Estonia would be Russian?

131

¹/₆ would be Russian

Fact!

A typical candy bar has about 280 calories. If you walk fast for 30 minutes you can burn about 80 calories.

If you eat 2 candy bars, how long would you have to walk fast to burn them off?

3.5 hours

What If?

The moon is 390,000 kilometers away. If you could drive to the moon at 70 mph, it would take you 142 days. The sun is 400 times farther away than the moon.

How many years would it take you to drive to the sun?

155 ½ years

What If?

The snack booth at the Wooly Worm Festival sells hot dogs for $1.25/$1.50 (with chili), French fries for 50¢/85¢ (large), and drinks for 50¢/$1 (large).

You have $3 and want a hot dog, fries, and a drink. What did you buy if you spent all your money?

134

a hot dog with chili, small fries, and a large drink

Weird!

Silkworms dislike noise and bad smells:
The smell of frying fish can kill a silk-
worm. No wonder silk is expensive!

For a silk kimono, you need 3½ yards
of silk. It costs $5.99 a yard. How much
will the kimono cost?

135

about $21.00

Really?

Jonathan Smith and James Kelly fought the longest boxing match ever recorded. The 1835 fight in Melbourne, Australia, lasted 6 hours 12 minutes through 186 rounds.

On average, how long was each round?

2 minutes

136

What If?

United States' Little Diomede Island is only 2.5 miles from Russia's Big Diomede Island.

If your boat can go 50 miles per hour, how long will it take you to go from Little Diomede to Big Diomede?

137

3 minutes

Cool!

Tanya finds the pair of shoes she wants at store A for $36.95. At store B they cost $45.00, but are on sale for 25% off.

Where will the shoes be cheaper?

138

store B, $33.75

Fact!

Spiders are not insects. Spiders have 8 legs and insects have 6 legs.

Lin has 12 bugs in his collection. All together they have 80 legs. How many insects does Lin have?

8 insects, 4 spiders

139

What If?

The Golden Gate Bridge of San Francisco is 4,200 feet long. San Francisco's Transbay Bridge is 2,310 feet long.

If you walked over both bridges both ways, about how many miles would you have walked?

140

about 2 ½ miles

Fact!

The 6 moon missions lasted for 192 hours, 245 hours, 216 hours, 295 hours, 265 hours, and 302 hours.

What was the average length in hours of a mission to the moon? How many days and hours did an average moon mission take?

$252 \frac{1}{2}$ hours or 10 days $12 \frac{1}{2}$ hours

Fact!

One metric horsepower is the energy needed to pull 4,500 kilograms 1 meter in 1 minute.

What would be the equivalent of 1 horsepower in pounds and feet?

1 horsepower pulls 9,900 pounds 3.28 feet in 1 minute

142

Really?

The Romans built 54,000 miles of roads and bridges. They had service stations (for horses and wagons) every 10 to 12 miles.

How many service stations were there on average?

143

about 4,900

Look!

Adam joined the book club at a bookstore and gets 20% off.

Adam buys 3 books, which cost $8.95 each. How much does he pay?

$21.48

144

Fact!

Your legs combined are about $^3/_7$ of your body weight.

If you weigh 105 pounds, about how much does each of your legs weigh?

145

$22 \frac{1}{2}$ pounds

Cool!

Charles Lindbergh was the first person to fly across the Atlantic Ocean alone.

He flew 3,610 miles in 33 ½ hours. How many miles per hour did he fly?

146

107.76 miles per hour

What If?

In 1990, the U.S. Mint made 12,031,422,711 pennies.

There are 17 pennies in a 1-inch stack. If all the pennies made in 1990 were placed in one stack, how many miles high would the stack be?

about 11,170 miles high

Really?

The largest hailstone ever recorded fell in Kansas and weighed 750 grams.

If 1 gram equals .035 ounces, how many ounces did the hailstone weigh?

148

26.25 ounces

Weird!

Spanish mailman Gabriel Grandos was sentenced to 9 years in jail for each letter he failed to deliver. Grandos failed to deliver 42,768 letters.

How many years long was his sentence?

149

384,912 years

What If?

You get a job babysitting on Saturday night. You watch the baby from 7:30 till 12:00 and earn $15.75.

How much do you get paid per hour?

150

$3.50 an hour

Look!

The Indianapolis 500 race track is 2.5 miles around (1 lap). The race is 500 miles, or 200 laps. The qualifying speed to enter the race is 224 mph.

If you qualified at 225 mph, how many laps did you make in one hour? Use a calculator.

Listen!

The loudest insect is the cicada, which can be heard ¹/₄ mile away.

If you were standing 400 yards away from some cicadas, could you hear them?

yes, ¹/₄ mile = 440 yards

152

Look!

Americans consume about 45% of their daily calories at dinner.

If you eat 2,300 calories a day, about what number will come from dinner?

153

1,035

Really?

The newest island is Pulau Batu Hairan, "Surprise Rock Island," discovered in 1988, north of Malaysia.

The area of the island is 1.9 acres. One acre is equal to 4,840 square yards. What is the area of the island in yards?

154

9,196 square yards

Weird!

The largest living organism is a fungus that covers 37 acres, weighs about 100 tons, and is 1,500 years old.

If 1 acre equals 43,560 square feet and 1 ton equals 2,000 pounds, how many square feet does the fungus cover? How many pounds does it weigh?

1,611,720 square feet, 200,000 pounds

Cool!

Prairie dogs live in large underground tunnel networks called towns. A 1-square-mile town can have a population of 16,000.

The largest known prairie dog town covered 25,000 square miles. About how many prairie dogs lived in this town?

400 million

Look!

You blink about 15,000 times a day, and each blink lasts about $\frac{1}{10}$ of a second.

How much time will you spend blinking in a day?

157

Fact!

In order to leave the Earth's atmosphere, a spacecraft must travel faster than 7 miles per second.

How many miles per hour must the spacecraft be going to get into orbit?

more than 25,200 mph

158

Who Knew?

The rhinoceros beetle, the strongest animal for its size, can carry 850 times its weight on its back. An elephant can only carry .25 times its weight.

If an elephant weighs 5 tons and a beetle weighs 8 ounces, how many pounds can each carry?

2,500 pounds, 425 pounds

159

Cool!

The hottest temperature ever recorded was 58° C in the Sahara Desert. The coldest temperature ever recorded was −89° C in Antarctica.

What are these temperatures in Fahrenheit?

160

136.4° F, −128.2° F

Really?

Ancient Mayan Indians measured the year at 365.2420 days long, which is not far off the modern measure of 365.2422 days. They were short only by 24 hours every 5,000 years.

About how many seconds were they short for every year?

161

about 17 seconds

Who Knew?

The Great Barrier Reef of Australia is the longest structure made by animals.

The reef is about 1,260 miles long. If there are 50 corals per foot, how many corals make up the reef?

332,640,000

Neat!

In 1890, a horse named Riley won the Kentucky Derby in 2 minutes 45 seconds In 1964, Northern Dancer won in 2 minutes flat. But in 1890 the race was 1½ miles, and in 1964 it was 1¼ miles.

Which horse was faster, Riley or Northern Dancer?

Northern Dancer

163

In the 4-year period from 1988 through 1991, NASA spent in millions $9,092, $11,036, $12,429, and $13,878.

How much did NASA spend on space projects in total from 1988 through 1991 to the nearest billion dollars?

$46 billion

Really?

A bee has 5,000 nostrils and can smell a flower 2 miles away. This is good because the bee must visit 156,250 flowers to make 1 ounce of honey.

How many flowers will 100 bees have to visit to produce 6 ounces of honey all together?

165

9,375 flowers

Fact!

Water boils at 212° F at sea level. The temperature at which water boils drops 1° F for each 550-foot increase in altitude.

A mountain climber is boiling water at 14,433 feet. At what temperature will the water boil?

a little less than 186° F

166

Who Knew?

The world's fastest creature is the peregrine falcon. The falcon can "power dive" at about 100 meters per second.

About how many miles per hour is the peregrine falcon's power dive?

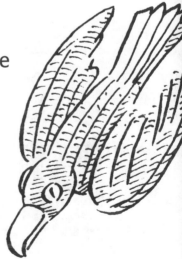

167

about 224 mph

Weird!

The California newt has a poison so strong that one drop can kill 7,000 mice.

If a mouse weighs 3 ounces, would one drop be lethal for a person?

168

yes, the mice weigh 1,312½ pounds, more than a person

What If?

Large tropical cockroaches can move about 40 body lengths per second.

If a cockroach is 1 inch long, how many miles per hour can the cockroach run?

169

2.27 miles per hour

Neat!

There are 911,000 miles of federal highways in the United States.

You are planning a car trip to travel over all 911,000 miles of the federal highways. You will average 60 mph, 10 hours a day, 5 days a week. How many years will your trip take?

170

about 5.84 years

What If?

Restaurants generally charge 3 times the cost of the food for items on the menu.

A restaurant pays $1.60 for a pound of fish, $1.80 for a dozen lemons, and 5¢ for parsley. If 4 fish dinners can be made from this, how much will each dinner cost?

171

$2.59

Who Knew?

A moth caterpillar eats 86,000 times its birth weight in the first 56 days of its life.

If the caterpillar weighs .001 ounce at birth, about how many pounds of food does it eat in the first 56 days?

172

about 5 ½ (5.375) pounds

Really?

A Boeing 747 carries 402 passengers and uses 3,464 gallons of fuel every hour.

If the fare were based on the cost of the fuel, and fuel cost $2.25 a gallon, how much would each passenger have to pay for a 3-hour trip?

173

$58.16

Fact!

Of all the planets, Mars is the most Earth-like. A Mars day is about 1 hour longer than an Earth day. A Mars year is 660 Mars days long.

How many Earth days are there in a Mars year?

about 687.5

174

Listen!

In the 2nd century B.C., the Romans kept 2 tons of gold in reserve. Today, gold is worth about $4,320 per pound.

How much would the Roman reserve be worth today?

175

$17,280,000

Really?

Lemon sharks grow a new set of teeth every 2 weeks. They grow 24,000 new teeth in a year.

About how many teeth make up a lemon shark's set?

about 923 teeth

176

Weird!

The Earth collects about 30,000 tons of space dust each day. This is about 12 ounces per square mile per day.

How many cups of space dust fall on each square mile of the Earth each week? 1 cup equals 8 ounces.

177

10¹/₂ cups

Cool!

Russia sold Alaska to the United States for $7.2 million. The Alaska Purchase was about 375 million acres.

What was the cost per acre, to the nearest penny?

178

2¢

Fact!

On the Richter scale, each number is 10 times as powerful as the previous one.

How many times more powerful is an earthquake that measures 7 on the Richter scale than one that measures 3?

179

10,000 times more powerful

Really?

The sun uses 4 million tons of hydrogen every second to keep shining. Fortunately, it has enough hydrogen to shine for 5 or 6 billion more years.

About how many tons of hydrogen will the sun burn in an hour?

180

about 14.4 billion tons

Weird!

What we call a billion the British call a milliard and what the British call a billion we call a trillion.

What would we call, in millions, the amount the British would call 2.5 billion?

2,500,000 million

Who Knew?

A sidereal year is 365 days, 6 hours, 9 minutes, 9.5 seconds. A tropical year is 365 days, 5 hours, 48 minutes, 46 seconds.

What is the difference between a sidereal and tropical year in minutes?

ALL ABOUT SIDEREAL

182

21 minutes

What If?

In Alaska, Myron Ace and 8 of his friends made a snowman as tall as a 7-story building. It took 13 days to finish the job.

If a story is about 9 feet high, about how tall was the snowman?

183

about 63 feet

Listen!

In 1816, the high temperature in Savannah, Georgia on the 4th of July was 46° F.

The normal temperature in Savannah on the 4th of July is 81° F. How many degrees colder than normal was it on July 4th in 1816?

184

35° F

Fact!

The New York Yankees won the World Series in 1956, 1958, 1961, 1962, 1977, and 1978. The Los Angeles Dodgers won the World Series in 1959, 1963, 1965, 1981, and 1988.

Which team won the most World Series from 1956 to 1988?

185

New York Yankees

Weird!

In 1846, 2 "dead" snails were given to a museum and glued to a board as an exhibit. In 1850, the staff noticed that 1 snail was still alive, and took it off the board.

The snail lived 2 more years. When did the snail finally die?

186

1852

Cool!

Elizabeth Taylor wore 65 different costumes in the movie Cleopatra. The cost of these costumes was $130,000.

What was the average cost of a costume? Use a calculator.

187

$2,000

Really?

The first person to raft down the Colorado River was one-armed geology professor John Powell. He traveled 1,000 miles down the river in 100 days.

If Professor Powell traveled 6 days of every week, how many miles did he average each traveling day?

about 11 1/2 miles a day

Fact!

People take about 12 breaths per minute, while mice take about 163 breaths per minute.

About how many breaths will you take in an hour? How many more breaths per hour will a mouse take?

189

720/hour; 9,060 more breaths

Neat!

Charles Blondin crossed Niagara Falls on a tightrope many times, including once blindfolded, once on stilts, and once carrying a man on his back.

The tightrope was 338 meters long. What is this in feet?

190

about 1,100 feet

What If?

Shifty Sam is to receive 1¢ the first day, 2¢ the second day, 4¢ the third day, and so on. Steady Steve is to receive 16¢ each day.

On what day will Shifty have been given more money than Steady?

ninth day

Weird!

There is a starch and plastic mixture called Super Slurper that can soak up 1,300 times its own weight in water.

How many gallons of water can 1 ounce (2 tablespoons) of Super Slurper slurp? There are 128 ounces in a gallon.

SUPER SLURPER

about 10 gallons